SPANISH FLY

A Spillage of Mercury

SPANISH FLY

Neil Rollinson

CAPE POETRY

Published by Jonathan Cape 2001

2 4 6 8 10 9 7 5 3 1

First published in Great Britain in 2001 by
Jonathan Cape
Random House, 20 Vauxhall Bridge Road,
London SW1V 2SA

Random House Australia (Pty) Limited
20 Alfred Street, Milsons Point, Sydney,
New South Wales 2061, Australia

Random House New Zealand Limited
18 Poland Road, Glenfield,
Auckland 10, New Zealand

Random House South Africa (Pty) Limited
Endulini, 5A Jubilee Road, Parktown 2193, South Africa

The Random House Group Limited Reg. No. 954009
www.randomhouse.co.uk

A CIP catalogue record for this book
is available from the British Library

ISBN 0224062077

Papers used by Random House are natural,
recyclable products made from wood grown in sustainable forests;
the manufacturing processes conform to the environmental
regulations of the country of origin

Typeset by Palimpsest Book Production Limited,
Polmont, Stirlingshire
Printed and bound in Great Britain by
Biddles Ltd, Guildford & King's Lynn

for Louise

Are those Corinna Brown's red panties
We see flying through the dark winter trees,
Or merely a lone crow taking home
His portion of the day's roadkill?

Charles Simic

CONTENTS

ACKNOWLEDGEMENTS

Acknowledgements are due to the editors of the following:

Football: Pure Poetry, edited by Ted Smith-Orr (Creative Energy), *Independent on Sunday*, *Last Words*, edited by Don Paterson and Jo Shapcott (Picador), *London Review of Books*, *New Writing 8* and *9* (Vintage), *Paris Review*, *Poetry London*, *Poetry Wales*, *A Quark for Mr Mark*, edited by Maurice Riordan and Jon Turney (Faber), *The Times Literary Supplement*.

'Constellations' won first prize in the 1997 National Poetry Competition. 'Deep-Third-Man' was highly commended in the same competition.

The epigraph by Charles Simic is from his poem 'Live at Club Revolution' taken from *Jackstraws*, published by Faber & Faber Ltd.

Many thanks to the Hawthornden Trust for a fellowship that allowed me to write in a Scottish castle for a month; to the Royal Literary Fund for another Writers' Fellowship; to the Society of Authors for a Betty Trask Award; to the Arts Council for a Writers' Award; to London Arts for the same, and much more besides; to Nick McDowell especially; to Annabel and David at Norden Farm Centre for the Arts.

Special thanks to the following folk: Michael Bayley, Louise Clarke, Paul Farley, Mark Haworth-Booth, Maurice Riordan, Robin Robertson, Henry Shukman, Matthew Sweeney and John Hartley Williams for all their help; the Mirash for the curries; and everyone at the East Dulwich Tavern for the beer and the inspiration. I hope that's everyone!

Thanks also to John Hartley Williams for the German: *Schaffst du nicht, du Wichser*, which translates roughly as: You'll never do it, you wanker!

THE PENALTY

The stadium comes to a hush;
it is so quiet you can hear a light-bulb
hum to itself in the dressing room.
You carry the ball in your hands,
your palms are sweating, you feel nauseous.
The goal-mouth rushes away.
You can just see, in the distance,
the white glow of the cross-bar,
the German keeper waving his arms.
You can hear him shouting:
Schaffst du nicht, du Wichser.
You settle the ball on its spot.
Do you place it, or blast it?
If you miss this kick you're finished,
your team-mates will sink to their knees
in the grass. You step back from the ball.
Schaffst du nicht, the keeper repeats.
You take a run. You are running all day
and night. When you get to the ball
you are weak with the effort.
You swing your leg, your foot
finds what you think is a perfect purchase,
the crowd goes wild, they rise in a wave
behind the goal. You watch the ball –
you can't believe where it goes.

THE RED LINE

How do I get to the Genito-Urinary clinic?
Take the red line, says the nurse,
and points through the door without so much
as a look of sympathy.
I wonder if she's heard what insidious practices
go on in there, or does she think
I have the clap, perhaps, and pity me?
It could be prostate cancer for all she knows.
I follow the red line through the sweltering hospital.
I roam the building's maze of corridors,
past orthopaedics, gynaecology; past theatre and mortuary.
I see many things on my journey: a doctor
laughing, two girls drifting hand in hand
like ghosts, the analgesic bloom of yellow tulips
dumped in a bin. Up above, you can sense,
in the tower-block of wards, the end of breath,
the simple flickering-out of people.
I wander on, following my ball of unwound wool
leading me where I do not want to go,
past the crematorium, into the outer reaches of the hospital
where nobody goes except the guilty and the soiled.
I pass the caretaker's hovel with its kettle steaming,
its mops and disinfectants; I pass the laundry house,
the boiler room. At the end of this line there's a place
where shrunken testicles float in formaldehyde.
I'm nearly there; a doctor is washing his hands in a sink,
the nurse is wearing a smile as she ushers me in.

MY WIVES

I descend on Holborn's escalator watching
my wives pass by on the opposite side,
smiling, waving at me; they shout
in Swedish, Russian, Urdu, that they'll always
love me. Even my English wives croon
in their dialects. My Japanese wives bow low,
their kimonos showering the stairs
with the scents of Hokkaido and Kanto.
My wives are everywhere – pacing the corridors,
rushing to Kilburn, Gatwick, Paddington,
smiling at me as they go. They have new
husbands now, waiting at home, but I know
it's me they miss. As we tunnel
the grim postcodes of Lambeth, Borough,
the Elephant and Castle, most of my wives
have left to catch connections for Kent
or Sussex. There are just the two of us now,
husband and wife for a couple of stops.
We sit in our seats, rocking in unison.
She twists her wedding ring, then
starts to weep. What can I do but join her?
We sob through Waterloo and Kennington,
all the way to Stockwell where she picks up
her bag, and slips through the doors.
I can picture her room in the Walworth Road,
her joss-sticks smouldering, that smell
of patchouli she's left in the empty carriage.
I go home alone, lie in an empty bed
while all my wives are sleeping with men
who do not love them.

FRUIT

Now that you've got me home, you hand me
the pinking shears with a grin. They are heavy
and cold like the ones my mother used to have.
You lie on the floor and ask me to cut you
free from your dress. So I take the hem
in my fingers, guiding the zigzag blades
with an unsteady hand, opening you up
to the waist, your legs pale in the lamplight.
I've wanted this all summer long, I can't imagine
how good you will be. I can smell your heat
like a fruit, hear your breath, deep and slow,
as the mouth of the shears slides
through your dress. I snip at the neck
and all the green silk falls off you like water;
I cut through your bra with a snap: your breasts
come free from their cups, their nipples like knots.
I run the blunt nose of the scissors over your lips
and throat, your belly and thighs, snick
the white of your knickers, and you part your legs
as I bring my mouth down to taste you,
dark and drenched like a flower in dew.
You play with my hair as I work with my lips
and tongue, and fingers, and you flood in my mouth
at last, pulling my head by the root.

CONSTELLATIONS

Beyond the house, where the woods
dwindle to a few stray trees, my father
walks on the lake with a hammer.

He's never seen so many stars,
and wonders why
with all that light in the sky

it doesn't cast a single shadow.
He takes a few blows at the ice, and drops
a sackful of bricks

and kittens into the hole, listens
a moment to the stillness of deep winter,
the hugeness of sky, the bubbles of warm

oxygen breaking under his feet,
like the fizz in a lemonade; the creaking
of ice as it settles itself.

His father's at home, coaxing voices
out of a crystal set, a concert from London.
Ghosts in a stone.

My father doesn't like that, he prefers
the magic of landscapes, of icicles
growing like fangs from the gutters of houses,

the map of the constellations. He turns on the bank
and looks at the sky, Orion rising over Bradford,
Cassiopeia's bold W, asking Who, What, When

and Why? And down in the lake, the sudden
star-burst of four kittens under a lid of ice,
heading to the four corners of nowhere.

NEIL ROLLINSON (1960–)

I am in revolt against your hyphens
Winston Churchill

It sends a chill down the spine finding it
in the index of a poetry anthology, that simple
hyphen with its intimation of mortality,

that knowing nod to some bleak point
in the future; its tail anchored in the sixties,
it head already sleeping in the next decade

or so. My very own *memento mori*:
a minus sign, a crossing-out, a simple gesture
of end, a blade across the throat,

that directorial slice of the hand – *cut!*
No mystical, far-eastern symbol this,
no ouroboros eating its own tail,

this is as straight as it comes, abrupt
and unequivocal, beginning and end, the road
to nowhere; and that blank space, waiting

for some clever dick to pencil the date in;
the monumental mason carving the final digits,
fixing me, once and for all, in the past.

THE SHIP

Eric and Dougie are glued to their glasses,
refugees from the hearth, wasted and sad.
I stand at the window watching the flood-rubbish
float downstream: a wardrobe, tables and chairs,
the branches of trees. You can feel the damp
in the stone floors, the pull of the current.
All the chairs are stacked on the tables.
It feels like the end of an era. It always does,
like a wake. Once a year, after heavy rain,
the moors empty their tributaries into the Ouse
and the pub sinks: a ship with its bar intact,
its pump-brasses glowing like gold, whisky
and gin, the bottles of old liqueurs standing
on shelves like medicines. We're shipwrecked
in the middle of York, the prospect of a week
at home drinking from cans; the wife and kids.
This is the family, the nearest and dearest,
Doug says, reading my mind. We fall into silence.
Rain beats on the windows, the mildewed coal
hisses and puffs against the damp. We're lost
in the booze, in the still moment before closing.
Fancy a lock-in? I ask. The landlord looks upstairs
like he's saying a prayer to the wife, then nods.
We'll be shut in the morning. He throws me the keys
and I head for the porch. I can hear the rain
beyond the door, the suck of the river against the step.
I can smell the green fields, the dry-stone walls,
the fells of limestone country come to town.

THE DRINK

He hated the water, and couldn't swim,
so when he walked backwards
over the wharf it was looking bad.
I rushed to the edge and stood there
watching him sink, his face under
the green water, his eyes staring, amazed
that anything could be so easy.
He looked calm, at home in this element,
his Crombie buttoned up against the weather,
his yellow scarf trailing down-current
like pond weed; a hand still gripping his pint.
A passer-by pulled off his boots
and jumped in beside him, got his head
from under the water, and dragged him out,
bumping him up the metal steps
like a piece of wreck, sitting him down
on a bench, and Doug said, *Thanks mate,*
I owe you a pint; and he hunched there, shivering,
clutching his glass, trying to light a wet cigarette
with a dud lighter.

FEATHERLITE

Waste not want not, you say as you
wring the last drops, the way
you'd get the dregs of the Burgundy
out of a wine box. You swallow the lot,
like an epicure, a woman who hasn't drunk
for weeks. I see the tongue curl
in your mouth, your lips sticky and opalescent
as it runs down your throat.
An elixir, that's what you call it,
your multi-mineral and vitamin supplement:
amino acids, glucose, fructose, vitamin B12
(essential for vegetarians), vitamin C,
magnesium, calcium, potassium,
and one third of the recommended
daily dose of zinc. You wipe your chin
with a finger, and put the tip to your tongue.
The taste is acquired; like whisky,
and anchovies, you develop a passion.
It's an aphrodisiac more efficacious
than rhino horn, or Spanish Fly,
it's delicious, you say, as you grab my hair,
and push your salty tongue in my mouth.

A BIG MAC AND FRIES

For the want of anything better to eat
I go to McDonald's for a Big Mac
and fries. When I ask for my order,
the girl behind the counter gives me
two Big Macs and fries. *It's an offer,*
she says, *two for the price of one.*
She smiles like it's my lucky day.
I don't want two Big Macs, I tell her,
I just want one. She looks anxious;
her training hadn't prepared her
for this. She shakes her head, she can't
take the burger back, it's mine,
I've paid for it; it's been accounted for,
she says, turning to the next man in line.
I carry my burgers down to a table
and scoop the limp bun from its greaseproof
paper. I still remember my first Big Mac,
the size of it, the gastronomic opulence
that years of Wimpys and fairground burgers
could never prepare you for: lettuce, tomato,
mayonnaise, and even a gherkin!
I mop my mouth with a serviette
and take the spare burger out into Holborn;
someone's bound to be grateful.
I offer it to the first guy I find
in a shop doorway. He shakes his head.
I haven't touched it, I tell him.
I'm not surprised, he says,
and asks for a cigarette.
I dump the box in a bin, where the burgers
are piling up nicely among the cans
and broken bottles.

PUDDING

(A exercise in cutting and pasting words and phrases
from a Mills & Boon 'Classic')

'It was one cliché after the other . . .'
Silent Crescendo

The table was laid: a basket of bread,
a bottle of wine, a copy of *Horse
and Hound*; the scent of steak
and mushrooms filled the kitchen.
When Raphael came in, stripped
to the waist, glistening with sweat,
Judith stared at the muscled torso,
the broad shoulders. She peeled off
her sweater and knelt before him,
I didn't make a pudding, she said,
and shook her head, sadly, she could
feel her nipples tensing, *but there's
stewed plums and cream in the fridge.*
She felt him harden beneath his jeans.
Is eating all you think about? he said
as Judith unzipped him. His arousal
was instant, Judith was stunned,
she'd never seen such a mammoth . . .
How's that? he said. *I thought you might
want something filling tonight.* She ran
her hand over the curve: a perfect specimen.
Eat as much as you like, he said
popping it into her mouth. She could feel
his pulse throb on her tongue, and a tremor
ran through her throat as she savoured
the first mouthful. This is delicious,
she thought, accepting the strong, hot brew.

Raphael moaned, his fingers moved
on her bare shoulders. She swallowed hard,
breathless and flushed, magnificent, she thought,
finishing the last generous mouthful.
She turned up her face for a kiss.
Judith that was superb, he said. *A toad is
lovely in a duckling's eye*, she replied, and
raised her mouth. *You could kiss me*, she said.
Yes, I'm beginning to realise that, he said
looking into her eyes, where flames were
literally burning.

LANDLADY

Watching her pull that pint
is an exercise in eroticism,
the way she grips the pump
and pulls, with a graceful, steady
stroke, her thumb rubbing the brass
nipple on top. I watch her biceps
clench and unclench, her nostrils flare
in the updraft of barley and hops.
A connoisseur, she licks her lips
and puts the glass on the mat
without a spill. As she bends
for the peanuts I sneak a look
down the front of her dress:
a glimpse of her breast, its bud
dark and alluring. I give thanks
for spring that brings girls
bra-less into the world again.
I can feel the lust, a sudden hunger
to touch her. Her body still winter-
white beneath her dress. I place
the coins in her pumping-hand,
still warm from the handle.
The beer is immaculate, a half-inch
of head, flush with the rim.
She keeps the best beer in town
and loves her barrels as much
as her husband and customers.
She studies my face as I sink
the first mouthful, and finds in it
the beer-blush of a happy man.

THE CURRY HOUSE

The brain, perceiving that the body has been injured [by the pepper's
chemical], secretes its natural painkiller, endorphin.
                                            Amal Naj, Peppers

So here I am again at the Gate of India,
under a painting of the Taj Mahal, waiting
for my fix. I gorge myself on poppadoms
and spoonfuls of chutney: hot mango and lime.
There are scallions chopped on a plate, a bowl
of pickled chillies to get me going.
I scour the menu for the most incendiary dish:
chicken jalfrezi, prawn vindaloo
or mutton phall, blind to the bhunas
and kormas, the sag aloos and brinjal bahjis.
I order the keema peas, with extra heat,
and soon it sits in a dish on its candle, wild
and simmering, a slick of ghee on the surface,
the birdeye chillies glowing like embers.
I close my mouth on a forkful of fireworks.
At first touch there's a conflagration,
my throat burning, my lips and gums seething.
The pores on my scalp open like a shower rose;
I suck at at the air, my mouth a gasping fumarole.
I drink glasses of Indian beer which is useless
for cooling the mouth – like pouring petrol
on a fire – but I won't touch the relish, the cool
raitha, for fear of spoiling the buzz, this light-
headedness. I can hear the banging of karahis
and baltis off in the kitchen, the rasp of a sitar
somewhere above me, the babble of conversation.
I'm high as a fakir climbing his rope.
I sniff my clothes, scented like Indian drapes,
my skin, with its odour of cloves and fenugreek,

that scent I'll sweat in the bed sheets tonight,
and come the morning, that last memento,
a glow on the ring, like a lover's kiss.

THE SEMIS

After a skinful of beer you become one
with the darts, bright as a monk fishing at dawn,
the treble 20 large as a lake.
Zen and the art of 501. You stand at the line
and watch the arrows spin through the smoke:
sixty, a hundred and twenty, one hundred and eighty!
The last match of the South London pubs'
semi-final and you're playing a stormer.
The corned beef sandwiches taste like salmon,
the beer like Veuve Clicquot, and even the barmaid
is stunning tonight. You preen your feathers, polish
the tungsten tips of your darts, and step to the mark.
You focus your mind: there is only the board,
the bull's-eye, blood-red and open, everything else
fades to a blur. A hundred and forty-two required.
You do your sums: treble 18, double 19, a bull to finish.
You see them off; the dart's instinct for flight
you imagine: neither a throw, nor a letting go.
They bed themselves in where you want them,
fifty-four, ninety-two, you watch the last dart home,
like a smart-dart, to the dead centre. Double bubble!
You're into the finals. You finish your beer
in a single gulp, and now you are through
your mind lets go. Your eyes glaze over.
You're seeing two doors to the gents, two platefuls
of sausage rolls, and two barmaids beaming at you
as you slide to the floor. You lie on your back
watching the ceiling-rose spin through the smoke,
a prayer wheel, a mandala cured in nicotine.

MASQUERADE

Disgruntled at the lack of work
and the free-falling nature of my bank account,
I have the bright idea of masquerading
as my fellow poets. I write to the festivals
with our biographies and rates.
I sign myself as Armitage, Riordan
and Burnside, thinking if I play this right,
they'll never know the difference.
In Leeds I'm a big success as a beardless
Matthew Sweeney, in Sunderland
I'm Don Paterson and get well paid, I'm
Hofmann, Maxwell, and Robertson,
I do Paul Farley and nearly get laid.
In a pub room in Dewsbury, Michael Donaghy
brings the house down with his Geordie accent.
I'm Ken Smith and John Hartley Williams,
I do the Martians, the New Gens, and any
number of famous but faceless American poets.
In Katowice I make a passable Kate Clanchy
on a fraudulent British Council trip.
I've never been so busy, I'm making quite a name
for ourselves, it's the new rock'n'roll,
everyone wants some. Tonight I'm here
in Manchester, giving a fine performance
of Neil Rollinson; he's never read so well –
you wouldn't even know us apart.

INTRUDERS

I knew they'd been here
the moment I opened the door;
I could sense a presence
around the flat,
ornaments displaced, a book
left open on the table.
The bathroom was warm,
the leaves of my aspidistra
dripping with condensation;
the towels were damp.
I found the knickers
on the bedroom floor,
a bottle of wine
beside the bed, half drunk,
two glasses, one with lipstick
smeared on the rim,
a condom draped on my pillow,
a glut of semen thick in its teat.
I found her wedding ring
laid on a pad,
a scribbled note in pencil,
See you around, you bastard.
That scent of hers
on the bed sheets again,
the window open, my ladder
propped against the sill.

CALLIOPE

with a line from Matthew Sweeney

Now that I've left, you're on the wine,
grumbling again you've lost your touch.
I'm not surprised, I gave you my best lines
and you left them on beer mats, or just
ignored them. Now that I've gone you're tired
of work, you struggle to find that smidgen
of class, that flash of insight I always inspired.
Singing, she pedalled over the moonlit bridge.
Remember that? I gave it away in the end.
You called me a slut and a whore,
said I was never there to give you a hand.
Look at you now, pacing the floor,
your paper blank, the pencils taking fright,
and your voice calling for me in the night.

The producer loves my work, he's a big fan,
but could I please read the poem
without the last few lines? Without
the last few lines! So half a poem, then?
We can't have words like that on the show.
But this is the Good Sex Guide, isn't it?
It's going out at 3.30 in the morning.
We have our advertisers to consider.
And I have my poem to consider,
beep out the words if you must,
I sweated ink for those last few lines.
We can't beep out, he says, *that only shows
there's something to hide.* Toyah is getting
exasperated, she thinks my poems
empower women, she wants one read.
These poems empower women, I say!
You can take it or leave it. So I read
the whole poem anyway after the dwarf
transvestite and the sado-masochist
do their spot, and he'll see what he can manage,
he'll talk to the folk upstairs, it's out
of his hands. When I turn on later,
I'm surprised; I look ten years younger,
handsome in make-up, and they run the poem
without a blip. I think about the perverts
up this late, sofa-bound, cock in hand,
waiting for the big one, and finding just poetry.
Or maybe they're waiting for the dwarf
transvestite and the sado-masochist
who are coming up next, right after the adverts.

FRENCH

Twenty minutes was all we'd manage
of compound tenses and conjugated verbs
before she'd lead me down the corridor
to her scented room, her joss-sticks,
and her threadbare *Tubular Bells*, for extra-
curricular activities beneath a poster of
The Grateful Dead. I remember the cool
expanse of her bed, her smell in the sheets,
her mouth, her short cropped hair,
and the taste of her skin when she came
to me, her nipples harder than stones.
I remember being pinned to the mattress
wondering if every woman was just like this,
amazed that anything could feel so good:
those minuscule breasts, the slope of her belly,
her cunt, so strange it made me tremble
just touching it. I couldn't get enough of that.
She was the girl from another world, everything
I'd never dreamed of, the way she loved it
from behind, wore nothing but Dr Marten's
on that big white bed – that turned me on –
everything about her did: the stud in her tongue,
her voice, the way she came – in French:
baise-moi, baise-moi. And afterwards her
taking the fee my folks could ill afford
for this private tuition, that was a turn-on too:
paying her week after week for the lessons.

THE LATE SHOW

We're deep into drinking time when Beardsley
starts the late show with a nutmeg, turns,
skins a defender – leaves him flat on his arse,
then swings the ball through a lens-blur
of emerald, where eight thousand zebras
are grazing in the Leazes End; they rise
in their seats, Ferdinand hangs in the air,
like Jesus beginning his slow ascension
to heaven, where the ball meets him, sweetly,
square between the temples. We're up
on our feet, screaming, watching the slo-mo's
pristine analysis over and over, the grace
of the movements, the undeniable beauty.
The keeper is nowhere; picking the ball from his net.
We stare at the box, you can smell the rain
deep in its circuitry, a whiff of the Tyne
from three hundred miles away.
The noise sweeps over us – the Toon Army,
the Magpies, the ranks of demented choristers
singing for their suppers. It's dark already
in Newcastle; here, as the whistle goes,
the last of the sun flares up in the bottles
behind the bar; it's warm, we sit with our beers
by open windows, running it through in our heads:
Shaka, Howey, Howey to Ginola, a shimmy, then crack:
the ball on its holiday, forty yards, the shine
of rain on the turf; Beardsley starting the late show
with a nutmeg, skinning a full-back, Ferdinand
up on his ladders, Jesus; you can hear the smack
of leather on head, see the grey blur of the ball
punching the net, the goalie flat on his back,
and still there's a touch of light gilding
the high windows of Marylebone.

We wait for our bus
and watch the pigeon
panic as the lights change.
It tries its wings briefly,
an old, arthritic angel,
but the wheel of a black cab
nips its rear to the Strand,
blowing its head
clean off, with a smack,
and a flurry of grey feathers.
Its circuitry
steams in the rain
like a bus map
for an unknown city.
We stare at the guts
like haruspices
looking for new ways home.
Except this is a map
for the tops of trees,
the ledges of office blocks
and the heads and shoulders
of the city's statues.

THE MILE-HIGH CLUB

Who can think of sex at a time like this,
in a toilet a mile up in the troposphere?
You won't find that in the *Kama Sutra*.

I sit in this cheap seat and rub my clammy palms
all the way from Gatwick to J.F.K.
30,000 feet above the grey Atlantic, every bump

and shudder sends my pulse racing:
the turbulence, the sudden pockets of air
that leave your stomach a hundred feet

above you in the clouds, the plane shaking
like an old bus on a dirt road. I close my eyes
and pray to a God who doesn't exist.

Anything can happen up here. I've read
the stories: the pilot's ten-year-old
flying the plane, a bomb in a suitcase,

a spark in the fuel tank, a suicidal steward
with a crippled daughter dying at home,
a man with a gun whose wife has left him,

the too-crowded skies we fly through;
a miracle we've got this far,
which after four hours is still 30° west

of nowhere, nothing between us
and the drink, and the seven miles below that.
Forget about joining the mile-high club.

I prefer it with my back on a mattress, a foot
above the solid earth, knowing if I fell
I'd only bruise an elbow or burn my arse

on the carpet, when the only turbulence
is the one we make of the mattress, our duvet
billowing like storm cloud as we ride the bed.

I bite my nails and count the minutes, I watch
a whole movie without understanding. I walk
the aisles like a lunatic pacing his patch of earth.

The only thing that stops me going nuts
is this unworldly beauty beyond the window,
the light on clouds, the pristine blue of the sky.

But what a way to go, you say, *the sudden*
cold as the plane breaks up. Imagine us falling
towards the featureless, cold sea, your hands

on my breasts, my legs wrapped around you;
we'd fuck the whole way down,
entwined like sycamore keys, our gasps

lost in the rush of air, in the vast
emptiness, in the perfect sky, while all around us,
buckled in seats, the dull and unimaginative

fall without sound. We'd hit the sea
at a hundred miles an hour, in mid-climax,
the water hard as concrete, our bodies

like two glass vases dropped on a floor,
shattered; without boundaries now, our fibres
drifting on the wave-tops, food for cod

and haddock, for sea birds crossing
the pond, hammerheads sniffing the current,
coming from miles for the big finish.

You don't have sex like that every day.
We circle in our stack above the airport.
Thank God for that, I think, you must have

lost your mind. And anyway, what could feel
as good as this, touching down with a jolt,
on terra firma, the weight of gravity

like an arm around your shoulder,
that feeling that you've got away with it,
that you've got away with your life.

A POEM ABOUT GOLF, DAVE

That looked like a slice to me, Al.
(Fred Haise to Alan B.Sheperd
 – Apollo 14 moon landing)

It's great to be out before Earthrise,
knocking the balls about, it keeps me sane,
keeps my feet on the ground as they say.
When you hit a ball up here it goes for miles:
you can see it glow, bright as a bullet
over the craters. An inspiration,
the drive of a lifetime. Dave on the other hand
sits in the capsule, brooding,
looking through telescopes, shaking his head.
It's a not a theme park, he'll say,
it's a sacred place. Dave's a poet.
Write a poem about golf, Dave, I tell him.
You might see something you never imagined.
But golf is no fit subject for a poem.

I watch the Earth rise every day like a glass marble,
silent, and stupid. I gaze for hours,
watching the brown smudges of Africa,
China, Australia. At night in the metal
hum of the landing craft, I dream of the green
fairways of Ballyliffin, the palm trees of Valderama,
the salty rain of St Andrews, the whole
moon's surface covered in grass.
I'll be home soon, the weight of gravity
dulling my dreams – a metaphor, Dave,
the arc of the golf ball falling short time after time,
the missed sitters, the cuts, the tops and
slices, and anyway, at the end of the day,
you need the practice, wherever you are.

ENTROPY

Your coffee grows cold on the kitchen table,
which means the universe is dying.
Your dress on the carpet is just a dress,
it has lost all sense of you now.
I open the window, the sky is dark
and the house is also cooling; the garden,
the summer lawn, all of it finding an equilibrium.
I watch an ice cube melt in my wine,
the heat of the Chardonnay passing into the ice.
It means the universe is dying: the second law
of thermodynamics. Entropy rising.
Only the fridge struggles to turn things round,
but even here there's a hidden loss.
It hums in the corner, the only sound
on a quiet night. Outside, in the vast sky,
stars are cooling. I think of the sun
consuming its fuel, the afternoon that is past,
and your dress that only this morning
was warm to my touch.

I give you a charmed, non-strange meson,
it disappears in the blink of an eye,
you give me a neutron, it falls to pieces
in minutes; I offer a pion, it decays in less
than a nanosecond. I ask for an axion,
a zeno, a Higgs boson, you say they are still
theories, they only exist in the mind.
You ask for a quark, I want to know
what flavour you'd like: truth or beauty?
I hand you a muon, a kaon, they vanish
without trace, you give me a microscopic
black hole, it evaporates before I can touch it.
You hold out your hands, but what can I give you
when nothing will last? I kiss your lips
and the heat of your mouth lingers a moment,
then disappears like everything else.

IN THE BATH

You step on the bathroom scales
and watch the dial spin back and forth
beneath the line, hesitant, reluctant
to settle. *I've put on half a stone,*
you say, in disgust, *how can you bear
to look at me?* I soak in the bath and watch
my beer-gut rise in the soapy water.
I tell you about the physicists at the bottom
of zinc mines, trying to weigh the cosmos
in tanks of pure water. They're looking
for dark matter, for WIMPs; for the missing
mass that will hold us together. The universe
it seems, is expanding inexorably.
We are growing further apart by the day.
You shake your head, and turn to face me.
I *can't believe it*, you say, *half a stone!*
I tell you you're beautiful, that you look the same
to me as you always have. You peel off
your knickers and climb in the bath. As you lower
your body into the suds and move against me
the water sucks and swells for a moment,
then floods from the lip, soaking the carpet.

(WIMPs – Weakly Interacting Massive Particles)

HAIR OF THE DOG

a poem ending with a line from Peter Redgrove

'A three-and-a-half hour's feast
with messages from Booze county.'

We sat by the window and drank;
a bright lunchtime in Cornwall.
A straightener he called it. Early doors
in the days when the pubs would close at three.
The drink was like medicine, every pint
leaving me clearer than the last, more wide awake.
I'd heard the stories of fist-fights, of broken
tables and chairs, this afternoon it was all talk:
magic and menstrual sex, poetry and the power
of dreams. His altar-piece sat on the table,
a black ceramic ashtray, the gin and slimline
spitting in its dead centre, the yoni and phallus,
he said, regenerative, fertile, sobering.
I should have been pissed, or dead
on my feet, but this was no ordinary drink,
this was the Duke of Burgundy out on the piss.
A gallon in three-and-a-half hours.
I could walk a tightrope, all the way
to Pendennis Castle, over the ships at their
moorings, the green-glass swimming pool
up on the hill. I could do it blindfold.
At half past three when they kicked us out,
we sat by the trawlers watching the town
turn crimson, the whole coastline, the sea
like a slick of blood, which was his colour,
and suited him; it turned his white hair red,
and just before we left I'm sure I saw him
bend his head and pop his glass eye out.

THREESOME

In the hour before dawn, when the smallest
sounds are amplified by the stillness,
before the first jumbos have skinned the rooftops,
Mandy wakes me again with her moans
from over the way, my early-morning call
for dawn, when the gardens are pungent,
the sycamores flushed with an unreal green.
As I stand by the window, I can see inside
her room, the parquet floor, the legs
of her bed, her curtains blowing, like veils.
In the house next door, Maureen
is drinking her tea in a dressing gown.
She wanders the garden, smelling the roses.
When she sees me standing there, naked
in morning glory, she waves, and slips the robe
from her shoulders, and stands like a wrinkled
Venus risen from her flowery gown,
her old brown body knotted, and faintly erotic
at such an hour. She starts to dance to this early
music, to the grace notes of lovers embracing
at dawn. I stand there and watch, tumescent
and spellbound, one eye on her and one
on the bedroom where Mandy is raising the roof
with her cries, an incantation to love, and Maureen
is stroking a huge, imaginary phallus, entreating me
to join this strange suburban rite, so I move
to the rhythm and blues of my strange neighbours,
and Mandy and I climax like lovers do, together,
and I come from the first-floor window
into the herb garden, and Maureen stands there
laughing, and clapping her hands in the sunshine.

EAST DULWICH

It is too quiet here, I can't sleep
for the silence. It's worse
than the country, at least there are
badgers and owls there, and sheep
chewing the lawn all night. It's totally
silent here, except, on the stillest
night with the windows open,
you can hear the town-hall bells
at Brixton counting the hours, then,
closer to daybreak, the pre-recorded
voice of a woman announcing: *The next
train to arrive at platform one will be
the 6.09 . . .* and: *This is East Dulwich.
Welcome to East Dulwich.*

A TIN CHURCH

We start the white-knuckle ride
on Dog Kennel Hill where the driver
puts his foot down at the bend
by the pub, Villeneuve in dreadlocks,
putting the bus through its paces.
We go full-tilt down Denmark Hill
grasping the greasy seats in front of us.
On every tight corner we lean,
forty strangers against each other's coats
in a single movement, graceful
as pillion riders. The world is a blur,
an abstract painting on each window.
At Camberwell Green the driver breaks
into song, a bluesy gospel fills the bus.
We chase the green lights
down Walworth Road, every bump
in the tarmac bouncing us
clean off our seats, the whole top deck
sniggering. We make the Elephant
in ten minutes flat. As we move
into George's Road a clutch of old ladies
who know the words take up the song
like the grey-haired ghosts of the Marvelettes.
Jesus is coming, hallelujah!
This is the way to travel, in a tin church
heading for town, with a congregation
of speed-freaks. When I get to my stop
at Waterloo Bridge they're in full-flow.
I stand on the pavement and wave them off
in a cloud of diesel and grit. I wonder
what they're on, and where they're heading,
or if they'll ever stop.

You can hear the monkeys,
the lone call of a jackal off in the distance
hippos, zebras, the rhino having its evening bath.
You can smell them too, downwind,
the faint, ammoniac whiff of urine
marking their private spaces.
I'm beyond memory now, sniffing the breeze.
For a moment I can feel the hairs on my body,
the atavistic pelt standing on end.
It is almost night, the sunset is turning
the leaves into embers.
As the lights come on in Camden Town
the penguins are putting their heads down
in their famous house, the giant turtle
sulks in its tank and sinks like a bathysphere.
A calm settles, like dusk in the Serengeti.
Even the weather is sympathetic,
scorching the city's grasslands these past weeks.
The last few stragglers are strolling
their curious dogs on Broad Walk,
taxis are passing on Albany Street,
a necklace of red buses circles the park.
I piss on a tree. It feels good.
I can smell the beer from lunch,
the malt and barley as it froths in the grass.
Tonight the foxes will smell me as they cruise
the back gardens of Primrose Hill,
my scents mingling with those of the cheetahs,
the lions, the chimpanzees.

WHITE CHRISTMAS

Having drawn the short straw in the Christmas rota,
he sits on the icy roof of the Weather Centre
watching the sky for the solitary snowflake
that will make this Christmas a white one.
He sips hot coffee from a thermos flask,
munches his way through a bait-box of turkey rolls,
and a slice of his wife's sad cake.

At four o'clock he watches the stars
from Hampstead to Crystal Palace flicker on,
but nothing by way of a snowflake. He sees
a meteorite or two, and every so often the quiet
track of a satellite crossing the sky. He wonders
if one of them might be a spy-in-the-sky,
if maybe somewhere, on a microchip,
in a Pentagon computer, there's a photograph
of himself sipping tea on a frost-covered roof?
He sticks two fingers up as they pass.

He yawns and closes his eyes for a moment,
they'll be showing old re-runs of Morecambe and Wise
on the telly, the kids will be fast asleep,
dreaming of empires of Lego, his wife will be making
her lonely way through a bottle of wine. Never mind,
he'll take her away when he picks up his winnings.

He has a whole month's wages on a white Christmas;
ten to one against, the bookies say, he can't believe his luck.
He's done his homework, his calculations, it all seems
clear enough, the barometer is already falling.
He scans the sky; a few pale wisps of cirrus
obscure the Pleiades: the start of a frontal zone
if he's not mistaken. He screws the top

off a hip-flask and takes a sip, he thinks about
sunshine. The Bahamas will be fine this time of year;
he can smell palm trees, he can smell tiger-prawns
grilling on charcoal; he can smell snow on the breeze.

SANTA CLAUS AS MACROSCOPIC QUANTUM
OBJECT DELIVERS HIS PRESENTS ON TIME

*It is a feature of the Quantum world that
particles can be in more than one place at a time,
provided that no one is watching.*
                                                    Henry Gee

As a macroscopic quantum object,
he moves at the speed of light, everywhere
at the same moment, in every chimney,
in every kid's bedroom, eating his billion
mince pies, drinking his copious dry sherries
at once. At a moment to midnight
he's in the skies over Oklahoma, Stockholm,
Tierra del Fuego, his reindeer and sleigh
like sudden lightning all over the globe.

If no one is watching, his quantum
wave-function will not collapse, and his work
will be done in the blink of an eye,
but all it takes is one little brat to lie in wait
beneath the bed, and Santa turns into Dad,
with a stick-on beard, and a silly hat,
staggering, half-cut into the bedroom.

But no one is watching, and Santa is filling
the Christmas stockings with dolls,
and jigsaws, Nintendos, and mobile phones.
He's home at the Pole almost before he has left,
with his feet up, sipping cocoa, the long, slow
year ahead of him, with toys to be made,
his reindeer fed and watered; he'll take things
easy now, take each day as it comes.

NO NETWORK COVERAGE

At twelve o'clock when the pubs
lock up, I climb the hill
to the graveyard above town.
There are loads of us here,
strolling among tombstones,
sat beneath the holly trees,
chuntering like mediums
in the cold night air. You can hear
the cheeps and chirrups,
like flocks of Arctic night birds
over-wintering among the angels
and stone goblets. There are snippets
of Bach, and Beethoven,
a disembodied mass filling the air.
I lean against a headstone
under the stained-glass windows,
a weathered inscription against my back.
I flip the lid on my mobile, call up
your number, and join the chorus.

HELPLINE

I love your calm, unhurried way, that sexy
lilt in your Irish voice as you take me,
line by line, through the nightmares
of my Autoexec.Bat and Config.Sys files.
We check the registry for clues,
the boot log, BIOS and System.Ini.
It's like love this language of DOS,
like talking dirty over the phone.
When I tell you it still won't work
you pause for a moment and moan,
like my hands have found the lush peripherals
beneath your anorak.
Well, you say, *it seems your system
is corrupt, you'll have to wipe
your hard disc now and reinstall Windows.*
I sigh down the phone. *Do you want me
to take you through it?* you ask.
You could make invalid page faults
and fatal exceptions sound romantic.
I look at your scribbled name on my pad.
Mary, take me gently, I'm all yours.

THE MECHANIC

There's nothing wrong with his car,
it's just somewhere to lie down
on a Sunday morning, away from the wife
and kids, flat on his back under the engine.
He lies there smoking a cigarette, watching
the world pass by at ankle height, a space
of his own – an hour or two to contemplate
the mechanics of peace and quiet,
the nuts and bolts and the gathering rust.
How slowly it grows. He feels the car's dead
weight above him, the idle power
of a hundred horses sleeping on all fours.
He studies its undercarriage, a total mystery,
caked in London's dirt and grime, a perfectly
white pebble wedged in the tyre tread.
He stares at the shock absorbers, the driveshaft,
and ponders the complexities of movement,
the magic of the internal combustion engine.
How does it all work? How does it get him
from A to B? His cup of tea cools beside him
on the kerb, cigarette smoke curls up the panelling.
When the kids call out, *dinner's ready*, he
stirs himself and goes indoors for the Sunday roast.
Later, it's Turtle-Wax and a yellow cloth,
he spreads it everywhere: over the bonnet and boot,
the handles and hubs, the lamps and fenders,
he lets it harden a while, then buffs it up
with his polishing mitts, while his wife looks on
through the kitchen window, washing dishes
and shaking her head.

DREAMTIME

We rock through a canopy of lime leaves,
a cargo of pungent secretaries lounging
in blouses, dozy bankers in mohair
cursing the weather; the cattle run, the 7.31
from Peckham to Putney. It's so humid
you could grow bananas in here. We snooze
in the heat, headphones hiss like cicadas.
By the Half Moon Tavern, a wasp, drawn
by a promise of sweat and the sweet
dampness of typists, flies through a window.
It lurches and swaggers, drunk on midsummer
pollen, up and down the aisle, everyone
wide awake now; a buzz of anxiety runs
through the bus. It hits the front window
and dithers a moment, dazed in the sunlight.
I wipe the sweat off my face and watch it
butt the window again, frustrated, the gardens
of Herne Hill pressed in glass, like his Permian
brothers sealed in amber. My neighbour rolls up
her *South London Press* and hammers it flat;
a yellow smudge on the glass, honey
and cider, the sweetness of local plum trees.
We breathe again, and doze in the hothouse.
The suburbs slide by like dreamtime,
all the way to Brixton where we rouse ourselves
and head for the Tube, yawning in unison.

OPEN ALL NIGHT

In the daylight glare of the strip lights
I wander past line after line of cornflakes
and tinned tomatoes, rice and biscuits,
not buying so much as out for a walk
in the hour before dawn, chasing the tail
of a poem that won't settle. What kind
of people go shopping at this time of day,
what strange addictions wake them
at four in the morning? It has the eerie still
of a catacomb, an Egyptian tomb stacked
with food for the afterlife. A stray starling
flutters its wings by the delicatessen.
I've never seen that before, it's unnerving,
like the soul of the just departed; maybe
it's me who has died and gone to Sainsbury's.
I can smell the fresh bread baking deep
in the store, a single chicken turns on a spit.
The till girls yawn and stretch their arms,
fridges hum from every aisle. I stroll along,
eating strawberries out of a punnet, I take
some milk and wander out; the dawn chorus,
missing a single starling, is in full throat
along the railway tracks. I can smell the gardens,
the summer jasmine, everything perfectly still,
and the poem finding itself at last, I can feel
the sentences fall into place. I'll leave it
for now, let it settle; there's a whole morning
to sleep on it.

BIG IN JAPAN

As I pass the gates of Buckingham Palace
I'm exposed in a hundred Japanese cameras:
a fossil, flash-frozen in Kodachrome.

I'm big in Japan, they've seen my face
blossom in a thousand Tokyo photo-labs.

In Wakayama somebody opens an album
to reminisce, and there I am under the apple tree,
part of the family portrait.

                A girl in Kagoshima
opens her purse by the sea and looks
at a photograph. It's a picture of me.

She can't remember my name, or how
she came to know me, but I'm smiling at her.

Behind my head she can see the traffic
in Parliament Square, the Abbey, the black hands
of Big Ben captured at ten-fifteen.

LONG EXPOSURE

for Phil Huntley

You're out all night in Dartmoor's freezing cold
and can't believe how silent it is, how dark
without a moon; you can hardly see
the boots on your feet. You sit on a stool,
the camera perched, owl–like, on its tripod.
The shutter is open all night, its aperture shrunk
to barely a pinprick, drinking the scenery
bit by bit. You think of the photons falling
invisibly onto the stock, like snow on a pond,
infinitesimal quanta of light fixing the landscape,
capturing detail you can only imagine
in this pitch–black scrub land.
You walk away for a cigarette, the single flare
of a match head could ruin your work.
At half past two you take a cloth and wipe
the condensation off the lens, knowing the camera
will make a ghost of you. You watch the stars,
and think of the Earth turning, you've seen
the Dog Star rise above the hill and fall from view,
you imagine the sun sweeping the globe,
the tide of dawn rushing towards you, already
over the Urals, the west of Afghanistan, people
rising for breakfast, and those in its shadow
drifting to bed, streetlights all over the western
seaboard flickering on. At five o'clock, before
dawn, you let the shutter fall, and pack your gear.
As you drive home you watch the first light
develop the moors, early sunlight racing west
across the frosted counties of England.

DEEP-THIRD-MAN

The infield is for wisecrackers, pepper-pots, gum-poppers:
the outfield is for loners, onlookers, brooders . . .
Stuart Dybek, 'Death of the Right Fielder'

I like it here, where the meadows of Kent
lap at the boundary rope, redundant
with apples and hops. You can ponder
the subtler things: the way a summer
ripens with every innings, sycamores moving
through deeper and deeper greens.
A man could drop dead out here
in the long grass, and no one would know.
They never found Blenkinsop, fielding
at deep-square-leg. They found some bones
the following year, his name carved in a tree,
but nothing more. We're a different breed.
Not for us, the tense excitement
of silly-point or forward-short-leg,
the flamboyance of bowlers
with their googlies and flippers.
I do bowl sometimes, for an over or two,
a languid, deceptive leg break;
but I pine for the stillness,
the silence of lost cricket balls
rotting like toadstools under a fence.
Nothing else happens, for months.
A whole season can pass
like a lifetime. I lounge in the sun,
practise my golf, or read a book.
You lose touch out here.
I watch the weather: the clouds,
the twelve degrees of turquoise
you find in an August sky,

46

and I love the rain, the way it soaks the hills,
the orchards, the whole of England.
One of these days they'll find me
dead among the dandelions,
the red smudge of a cricket ball
gracing my head, or maybe I'll disappear
into the unmown grass, the oaks
and elm trees, the last day of summer,
into memory, and beyond.